The *Explorer* steaming up the Colorado in 1858.

RIVERS OF THE WORLD

the
Colorado
MOVER OF MOUNTAINS

by Alexander L. Crosby

Maps by René Martin
Drawings by Evelyn Urbanowich

THE GARRARD PRESS
CHAMPAIGN, ILLINOIS
80325

THIS BOOK WAS EDITED AND DESIGNED
UNDER THE SUPERVISION OF NANCY LARRICK, ED. D.

The author and editor are indebted to these persons and agencies for assistance in checking the accuracy of this book: WILLIAM H. GOETZMANN, assistant professor of history, Yale University, author of *Army Exploration in the American West 1803-1863;* AGNES CREAGH, director of publications, Geological Society of America; Bureau of Reclamation, Department of the Interior; and the Atomic Energy Commission.

The Animals of the End Papers

Prong-horn antelope by E. P. Haddon
Black-tailed prairie dogs by E. R. Kalmbach
Clark's swift by E. P. Haddon
Badger by E. P. Haddon
Boyle's king snake by E. P. Haddon

All from U. S. Fish and Wildlife Service

Bureau of Reclamation

Joshua trees in Arizona.

Contents

THE COLORADO
and its main tributaries

1. No River Like It

For 12 million years the Colorado River has been moving mountains to the sea. Its name, given by Spanish explorers, means *colored* or *red*. The name has been well earned. On an average day the river carries one million tons of silt through the Grand Canyon. This is enough mud to fill a string of gondola cars stretching 140 miles, from Philadelphia to Washington.

Every quart of water in the Colorado carries 11 teaspoons of silt. No wonder that old-timers say the river is "too thick to drink, too thin to plow."

There is no river like the Colorado. It has made a world record for wearing down mountains and carving canyons.

The Colorado begins as a clear stream in the Rocky Mountains of northern Colorado. This is country where the evergreens are tall, where the aspens make shining patches of gold in autumn. Elk roam through the forests, and beavers build their dams across hundreds of streams.

The winter snows are deep. When they melt in the late spring, every mountain ravine echoes with a rushing brook. The brooks join to form thousands of white-foamed creeks. The creeks join to make raging rivers, tumbling rocks along their courses.

The rivers pick up sand, gravel and soil from their banks and from the creeks. All of these muddy torrents join the Colorado on its 1,400-mile journey to the Gulf of California.

Once it leaves the Rocky Mountains, the Colorado becomes a river of the desert. And the desert is where the Colorado has done its most spectacular work. The great river and its tributaries have lowered the level of the land by thousands of feet. They have left towering buttes and spires of harder rock. They have slashed the level plateaus with canyons as deep as a full mile.

Grand Lake, headwaters of the Colorado River.

All of the loose soil and rock particles have been carried south by the Colorado. The river's load has been dumped into the Gulf of California or spread on the lower desert in flood time.

The Colorado has been able to eat away the mountains of the desert because they have little or no protection. There are no forests and grassy meadows to hold the water and the soil. The desert doesn't get enough rain to grow woods and grass.

Cactus clumps and skimpy bushes are not enough to hold the soil. So when rain does come, the water runs off quickly. It washes as it runs. It scours the land to the bare rock. Even the rocks finally wear away as the gritty streams work like sandpaper.

Rails and highway follow the river in Glenwood Canyon, Colorado.

Frost and wind help the streams and rivers attack the rocks. The frost gets into tiny cracks and splits the rocks. The wind hurls grains of sand against the bare surfaces. You can't see any

8

change in a rock wall from one month to the next. But over thousands of years the changes are enormous. Over millions of years the changes are unbelievable.

Think of the Grand Canyon, the Colorado's biggest excavation. It is a mile deep, 4 to 18 miles wide and 217 miles long. If every building in the United States were dumped into the Grand Canyon, this great hole in the desert wouldn't be half filled.

The Colorado is a lonely river. It runs through wild country that hasn't been fully explored. There are only three sizable towns on its whole length: Grand Junction, Colorado; Moab, Utah; and Yuma, Arizona.

When the Colorado enters the desert country, it travels alone. There is no room along its banks for highway or railroad. For many miles the river runs between rock walls two or three times higher than the Empire State building. The walls are almost vertical.

Some rivers are as calm and dependable as a well-bred cow. Not the Colorado. It may be just a muddy stream in the dry months of late summer, fall and winter. But when the snows melt in the mountain ranges of Colorado, Wyoming, Utah and New Mexico, the river becomes a roaring flood. It carries 125 times more water than it does at the low mark. It rises as much as 115 feet in the Grand Canyon.

For centuries the only people who knew the mysteries of the Colorado were the Indians. Some tribes had cliff dwellings in the rocky walls. Others built crude huts in the deep canyons that led down to the river. The Indians chiseled trails through these canyons, hugging the sides of dizzy precipices. And the Indians knew the few places where the river could be safely forded.

The first whites to visit the lower Colorado were Spanish missionaries and soldiers. They arrived less than 50 years after Columbus had found the New World. In the early 1800s the river was crossed at several places by trappers, traders and Mormons.

But no real exploring had been done by 1848, when the United States took the Colorado country and California from Mexico. No white man had gone to the bottom of the Grand Canyon and very few had seen

The Colorado carves the desert at Dead Horse Point, Utah.

it. The maps of that period only guessed at where the river ran.

Bloody chapters of frontier history were written in the Colorado country. The little settlement of Lees Ferry, just south of the Utah boundary, is remembered for Major John D. Lee. He was a fanatical leader of the Mormons in 1857 when the United States sent troops against these persecuted people. At Mountain Meadows on the Old Spanish Trail, more

11

than 100 miles west of Lees Ferry, a party of about 140 emigrants had camped on their way to California. Paiute Indians attacked. For three days the emigrants fought back from behind their wagons.

Then a group of armed Mormons came up under a flag of truce. The Mormons offered to take the party to a safe place if they would leave their guns behind. The offer was accepted. But at a command from Major Lee the Mormons and Indians shot down the emigrants. Only a few children were spared.

Lee fled to the Colorado River. He built a stone hut and hauled logs 60 miles to make a raft big enough to carry horses and wagons across the river. Nineteen years later he was found at the ferry and arrested. After two trials, he was convicted and shot at the scene of the massacre. The Mormon Church declared he had had no authority to order the killings.

The rafts and ferries used by the emigrants have long since disappeared. Today the Colorado is crossed by railroad bridges, highway bridges, the great Hoover Dam and seven smaller dams. Yet there are hundreds of miles between some bridges. Highway maps of Utah and Arizona show roads that lead to

The V-shaped gap (top left) is Hole-in-the-Rock. In 1880, Mormons took 83 wagons through the gap and then crossed the Colorado River.

the cliffs above the river and then make a final stop.

Below Yuma the Colorado enters Mexico. The river runs 80 miles through low-lying desert to reach the Gulf of California. Fishermen and other boatmen on this stretch have learned to fear a tidal wave called a bore. Tides in the Gulf of California run as high as 32 feet. One of these high tides can build a wave 15 feet high which booms up the river at 35 miles an hour. Boats have been overturned and many passengers drowned by these gigantic waves. Fortunately, there are not many boats and the waves seldom run 15 feet high.

The Colorado empties into the Gulf of California at a desolate spot. There is no town. There are no wharves with ocean freighters. Only a few fishermen's shacks mark the end of the river that moves mountains.

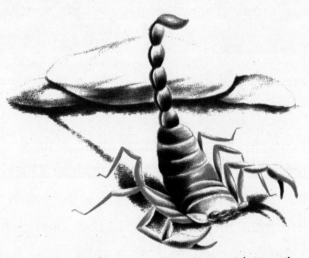

A desert scorpion stings with its tail.

2. The Cruise of the *Explorer*

For more than 100 years, trappers, prospectors, surveyors, photographers and seekers of adventure have braved the Colorado in small boats. Nearly all went downstream because a boat could not be pushed upstream through the terrifying rapids. No one knows how many were drowned. The successful voyagers often found wrecked boats and sometimes a body.

The dangers of the Colorado were real. When explorers entered the dark and narrow canyons, they found walls so high the sun could not be seen. But there was no turning back and no way out for many miles. If the boat struck a rock, repairs had to be made with anything that could be found. If food was lost in the river by an upset, the boatmen ate less.

The worst rapids could usually be dodged by what was called "lining" the boat. All equipment and supplies were first taken out and carried ahead along the rocky bank. Then a line was tied to the bow of the boat and another to the stern. One man took the lead line and picked his way through the rocks on shore while his partner held the stern line. Thus they guided the empty boat through the rapids. But sometimes the strong current would toss the boat so wildly that one of the linemen would be dragged into the river.

Where the canyon walls gave no foothold, the only course was to ride the rapids, trying to steer with an oar. Waves often covered the boatmen and tore the oars from their hands.

One of the earliest attempts to explore the Colorado was made in an iron steamboat, traveling *upstream*. This was the famous cruise of the *Explorer*, in charge of Lieutenant Joseph C. Ives of the army's Topographical Corps. A large party of scientists, soldiers and packers went with Ives.

The young lieutenant was sent to the Colorado in 1857 because the United States government expected to have a full-scale war with the Mormons of Utah.

Lieutenant Ives saw plenty of jack rabbits.

How could the troops be supplied? There was no railroad to Utah, and the wagon roads were hopeless in winter. Would it be possible to haul supplies by boat up the Colorado, and then overland to Utah?

Ives had to answer that question. But his party would do more. The scientists would study and map the unknown country. They would make reports on the weather, on the Indians, and on the plant and animal life.

A 54-foot steamboat was built for Ives in Philadelphia. It was made in sections so it could be taken apart for an ocean voyage to Panama, and then carried across the Isthmus of Panama by railroad. On the Pacific side it was loaded on another steamship for

San Francisco. There it was transferred to a small sailing vessel going to the mouth of the Colorado.

Putting the boat together on the sticky mud flats of the Colorado delta looked impossible. But Ives's men dug a big trench and lined it with old logs carried down by floods. In this cradle they bolted together the *Explorer*. Then they waited for a high tide.

The high tide came a month after the landing. The bright red steamboat floated. Stoked with driftwood and dead branches from the shore, the *Explorer* slowly steamed up the river to Yuma.

Yuma was then little more than a fort, a store, a blacksmith shop and a saloon. At the fort Ives met other members of his party who had come overland from San Diego and San Pedro. On January 11, 1858, with 24 whites and two Indian guides aboard, the *Explorer* headed north into unknown country.

The river was very shallow at that time and the ship was grounded on sand bars several times a day. To get by a sand bar, men waded ahead with anchors and lines. The anchors were made fast in the sand and mud. Then the lines were slowly wound on a windlass, pulling the ship forward.

The *Explorer* in Mojave Canyon of the Colorado, as sketched in 1858.

This system was very funny to the Indians. They could travel much faster afoot or on small rafts pushed with a pole. Groups of Indians would run ahead of the boat and gather opposite hidden shoals so they could get a good laugh when the boat grounded. Captain Robinson soon learned that wherever the Indians waited, there was trouble in the river. At last the Indians took pity on the poor whites and began to point out where the water was deepest.

Each evening the explorers made camp on shore, since this part of the Colorado was in open desert country. Indians came regularly to look at the strange whites and to trade. One scientist persuaded Indian children to gather live specimens for him, rewarding them with beads for lizards and pouched mice. The children were sure he ate them.

Two months after leaving Fort Yuma the *Explorer* reached the lower end of Black Canyon, about 40 miles below the site of Hoover Dam today. The party had traveled 200 miles in a straight line but the twisting river made the distance much greater. Ireteba, a friendly Mojave guide, warned that the boat could never get through the fearsome canyon ahead. He said the channel was filled with huge rocks through which the water dashed furiously.

The Indian was right, although the *Explorer* never had a chance to breast the rapids. At the mouth of the canyon the ship struck a hidden rock so hard that

20

several men were thrown overboard and the boiler was torn loose. Luckily, no hole was made in the iron bottom.

Repairs were made in three days. But Ives decided it would not be practical for any steamboat to navigate the Black Canyon. So the *Explorer* was turned around for a 30-mile run down the river to Cottonwood Valley, where camp was made.

A mule train with supplies from Fort Yuma was long overdue. For days the men had been living on corn and beans bought from the Indians, and every stomach was complaining. Ives had another worry. The friendly Mojaves were no longer friendly. One night they tried to set fire to the dry grass around the camp.

Through one of the Indian guides, Ives found out what the trouble was. The Indians had been told by the Mormons that the explorers were going to take their lands.

Nervously Ives and his men waited in camp for the supply train. One night a white man called across the river for a boat. The skiff was sent to get him. The stranger said he was an emigrant, bound for California. But one man in the Ives party recognized him as a Mormon bishop from Utah. He was a spy.

Instead of throwing him out of camp, Ives gave him corn and beans and two blankets for the night. Unknown to the lieutenant, another Mormon was hidden in the bushes by the edge of the river. This was Jacob Hamblin, the famous scout. He was trying to get the Mojaves and Paiutes to attack the party.

Ives outwitted Hamblin by talking to Cairook, the Mojave chief. Cairook believed Ives when he said the party did not want the Indians' lands and would soon leave. Good feelings were restored. Best of all, the supply train arrived and the men ate like happy pigs.

A mountain sheep of the Grand Canyon area.

3. The Grand Canyon

The Indians had told Ives about the Big Canyon of the Colorado, many miles northeast of the Cottonwood Valley camp. The young lieutenant was determined to see it. He divided the party into two groups. One would go back to Yuma on the steamboat. The other would head overland with more than 100 pack mules to the Big Canyon. Ives led the land party, which had 20 soldiers under Lieutenant Tipton.

23

Ireteba, the faithful guide, was badly needed. But he would not enter the country of enemy Indians. He managed, however, to find a pair of Hualpais Indians who would guide the party to watering places and passes. One looked so ugly and villainous that one of the scientists said he should be pickled in alcohol as a zoological specimen.

After 10 days of crossing mountains and valleys, the party climbed to a broad tableland. Herds of deer and antelope dashed away. To the north could be seen a long line of bluffs, the northern rim of the Grand Canyon. Ives was so excited he stood still, admiring the scene for a long time.

The guides were impatient. They started down a narrow and precipitous ravine. It was hard for the mule train to keep up with the sure-footed Indians as the trail led down, down, down. Other canyons branched off. The canyon walls became higher and higher. Then the scene changed, as Ives wrote in his journal:

Huts of the rudest construction, visible here and there in some sheltered niche or beneath a projecting rock, and the sight of a hideous old squaw,

There was no Bright Angel Trail to the bottom of Grand Canyon in 1858.

staggering under a bundle of fuel, showed that we had penetrated into the domestic retreats of the Hualpais nation. Our party being, in all probability, the first company of whites that had ever been seen by them, we had anticipated producing a great effect, and were a little chagrined when the old woman, and two or three others of both sexes that we met, went by without taking the slightest notice of us.

25

After traveling down the canyon 17 miles, the party came to a branch canyon with a sparkling stream and plenty of grass. Men and mules rejoiced, and camp was made for the night. Ives named the stream Diamond River.

The next morning, April 4, Ives hurried down the stream and followed it around a bend. Suddenly the Colorado River was before him. Ives was probably the first white man to reach the bottom of the Grand Canyon, and he knew he was making history.

At this point the Colorado was about 150 feet wide. The water roared past the rocks. Although the canyon walls were lower than those farther east, they were high enough to make a man feel like an insect.

Ives and the scientists spent a day exploring, sketching and studying the layers of rock. The next morning the Hualpais guides led the party up through a maze of canyons to the high plateau. They warned that no more water would be found for three days. Then, during the night, they disappeared.

To plunge into the unknown desert above the Grand Canyon without guides was perilous. But Ives had no other choice. The pack train moved on.

Two days later the need for water was desperate. Ives found an Indian trail leading down a canyon. There might be a spring or creek below. Men and animals started down the trail, which soon became a narrow ledge. Below them a precipice dropped 1,000 feet. A sheer wall rose above. Ives's mule was walking only three inches from the edge. Some of the soldiers got so dizzy they had to crawl on hands and knees.

Luckily the giddy trail widened at one point into a shelf where the mules could be turned around, for they could not go farther. To save the animals, Ives had their packs removed. He ordered the Mexican herders to take the herd back to the last watering place.

Ives himself led a party of 15 men farther down the canyon. After 13 miles they came to a stone cliff 40 feet high, where the path seemed to end. But Baron Egloffstein, the artist of the expedition, discovered a half-rotten ladder made of sticks and bark. He started down it. One side gave way completely, but the Baron made a fast slide down the other side to the bottom. Farther down the canyon he found a village of Yampais Indians.

27

Engraving from Powell Report

An Indian village in the Grand Canyon region, as drawn 100 years ago. Basket in the center was used in gathering seeds.

Getting the Baron up the cliff was a problem, since he was no lightweight. The soldiers knotted the slings of their rifles together to make a rope. The Baron was hauled up safely.

The geologist of Ives's party, John Strong Newberry, was probably the first man to grasp the ancient history of the Colorado River. Since then, the story has become much clearer. Millions of years ago the Colorado plateau was the bottom of an ocean. Slowly the land was pushed upward above the water. The ocean disappeared.

But the river from the high mountains of the north had to find its way to the sea. It kept grinding away at the rock in its path, cutting a channel deeper and deeper as the land rose. Small streams from the plateaus on both sides of the river carved smaller canyons. Frost cracked huge rocks, and sandy winds chiseled others. In many places great sections of rock broke loose because of cracks left when the rock was formed.

Always the hardest rocks resisted erosion. That is why the Grand Canyon is dotted with soaring pinnacles and buttes. These monuments of stone remind many people of cathedrals and skyscrapers. But a real skyscraper would be a little thing if placed in the Grand Canyon.

The rock walls of the great canyon are a clear record of the earth's history. Geologists can read the record as easily as we read a newspaper. They know when each layer of rock was formed and what minerals colored it.

All of the layers have been named, often after the

Indians of the region. Thus the top layer is white Kaibab limestone. Then come gray Coconino sandstone and red Supai shales. Below them are blue-gray Redwall limestone, green Tonto shale and basal limestone. After three more layers the river cuts to the very crust of the earth, gneiss and granite, at the bottom of the gorge.

This record of rocks goes back two billion years. There is nothing like it anywhere on earth.

These shell and fern fossils were among hundreds of specimens collected by Dr. Newberry, the geologist with Ives. Sea shells show that an ocean once covered the Colorado plateau.

4. The Wonderful Hopi Villages

After exploring the country south of the Grand Canyon, Ives turned toward the east. His destination was Fort Defiance, an army post near the present boundary between Arizona and New Mexico. He would have to cross the country of the savage Navahos. And there would be no Indian guides to find the few water holes.

For two days the party straggled along under a burning sun. Water kegs and canteens were emptied. The mules were in wretched shape. "Too thirsty to graze, they stood all night about camp, filling the air with distressing cries," Ives wrote. "This morning the weakened brutes staggered under their packs as though they were drunk."

31

If the mules died, the men would have a poor chance of getting out of the desert.

Ives kept looking for some break in the level plain. Suddenly the party came to a ravine. Fresh bear tracks led down it, and the men's hopes soared. Wild animals knew where to find water.

Turning down the ravine, the party soon came to a large pool of good water. The mules plunged in and drank and drank.

The grizzly bear whose tracks had helped to save the party was seen nearby. As he tried to get out of sight, he was riddled with bullets. That evening the menu was bear soup and bear steak.

After some rough traveling the party reached the northern base of Bill Williams Mountain. This country seemed like Paradise. The volcanic rocks held plenty of water from melted snows, and there was good grass for the mules. But the animals were in bad shape. Sharp rocks had worn away their shoes and were bruising their feet. Army saddles had rubbed patches of skin from their backs.

To save the mules, Ives decided to send Lieutenant Tipton straight on to Fort Defiance with most of the animals and men. But Ives wanted to see the seven fabled villages of the Hopis, somewhere to the north. Built of stones and clay like the cliff dwellings, these towns or pueblos were far ahead of the huts that other Indians made with earth and branches. Spanish missionaries had visited the pueblos more than 200 years before, but there were no records since.

For this side trip, Ives chose 10 men and the mules that were least worn-out. The first obstacle was the Little Colorado River, a tributary of the big river. But the party was prepared. A collapsible Buchanan boat was unloaded from one of the mules. Made of canvas with a light frame of pine, it could carry 12 men.

The next obstacle defeated the men and mules. It was the Painted Desert, with not a tree, not a shrub, not a blade of grass. As the sun went down, scorpions, tarantulas, centipedes and rattlesnakes came out of hiding to enjoy the cooler air. Deciding it was hopeless to push through this parched and dusty region, Ives turned back after a day's march.

The party then followed the Little Colorado River south for some 25 miles. A well-beaten Indian trail was found, leading toward the blue peaks of distant

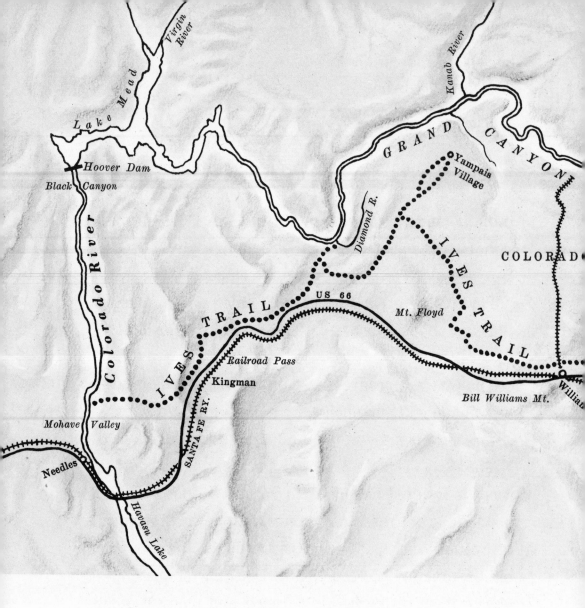

mountains. Happily, there were enough springs along
the way to keep the mules moving.

When the sun went down on May 10 and the hazy
air became clearer, Ives studied the bluffs ahead with
a spyglass. Suddenly he saw what he was looking for:

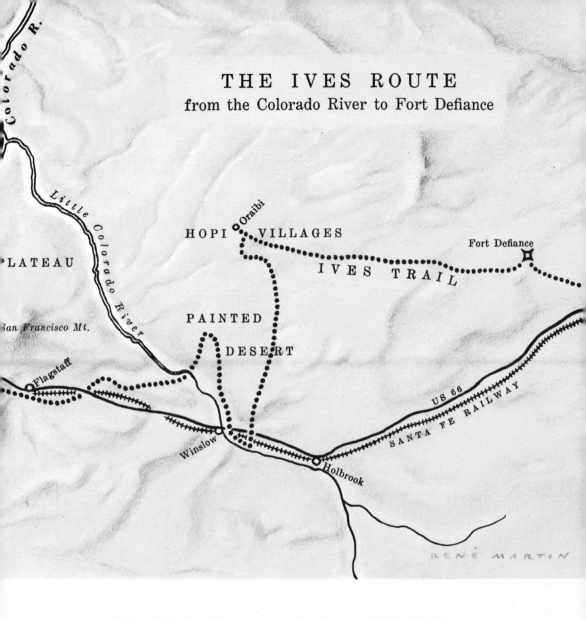

THE IVES ROUTE
from the Colorado River to Fort Defiance

Colorado R.

Little Colorado River

PLATEAU

San Francisco Mt.

Flagstaff

HOPI Oraibi VILLAGES

Fort Defiance

IVES TRAIL

PAINTED

DESERT

US 66

SANTA FE RAILWAY

Winslow

Holbrook

RENÉ MARTIN

two of the Hopi villages, perched on a high bluff some eight miles ahead.

The next morning the party took the trail eagerly. There was no sign of life until two Indians, riding one small horse, came charging down a hill. Shouting a welcome, each Indian shook hands with every man in the party. One carried an ancient flintlock musket. He wore cotton trousers, a blue coat and a belt of round brass plates. Both men were unusually neat, with carefully combed hair.

Thirty or forty more Indians came running from the pueblo, and they shook hands all around, too. Ives explained in sign language that the mules needed water. The Hopis led the party up the steep slope. Soon they came to a crowd of Indians gathered around a small, round reservoir, lined with masonry. A pipe from the top of the mesa filled the basin with cold water.

When the mules were satisfied, the party climbed higher to a second reservoir, used for drinking. Terraces had been built on the face of the bluff for vegetables and peach trees. All of the terraces were irrigated.

The Hopi chief, a pleasant man, took the explorers up a long flight of stone steps to the pueblo. The village was almost square, with a high stone wall for defense against the Navahos and other enemies. A ladder led to the top of the wall. Stone steps went to

Ives's camp on the Colorado plateau, on the way to the Hopi towns.

a higher level, where doors opened into a number of adobe houses.

The chief invited Ives and two of his companions into his apartment and asked them to sit on skins spread near the wall. His wife brought refreshments: a jar of water and tortillas, which were thin sheets of corn meal, baked on hot stones and rolled up.

Ives was impressed by the cleanliness and neatness of the room. Skins, bows and arrows, antlers, clothing and ornaments were on shelves or pegs. Vases, flat dishes and gourds filled with meal or water stood along one wall. A fireplace and chimney were in one corner. Ears of corn were piled in an adjoining room.

Ives spread out a map of the Colorado country. The chief pointed out the locations of the six other Hopi villages. Next the lieutenant made a bargain for several sheep, to provide food. Each sheep was paid for with one blanket.

The visitors climbed another flight of stairs to the roof, where they had a magnificent view. They could see five trails in straight lines, one of them the Navaho trail to Fort Defiance.

Modern Navahos in a war dance at Page, Arizona.

Bureau of Reclamation (A. E. Turner)

Ives invited the chief and two of his friends to visit his tent on the bluff below. This time the refreshments were bread and molasses. Almost instantly the tent was jammed with hungry Hopis.

The ancestors of these Indians were the cliff dwellers of Utah, Colorado, Arizona and New Mexico. Why the cliff dwellings were abandoned is unknown. There is a legend that hostile Indians drove the cliff dwellers from their strongholds and into the Colorado River, where they turned into fishes. The Navahos still won't eat fish from that river.

Today the Hopis are known for their famous snake dance, held in August to bring rain. The dancers belong to the Snake and Antelope secret societies. While the Antelope priests shake rattles, the Snake priests dance with snakes in their mouths. Then the snakes are turned loose in the desert. They are supposed to carry prayers for rain to the gods.

One of the Hopi pueblos is Oraibi, which is the oldest town in the United States. Oraibi was visited by Ives before he started for Fort Defiance.

The final journey to Fort Defiance went smoothly. Eight of the Hopis traveled with the explorers, guiding them to springs and streams and grassy spots.

More Hopis joined the party along the way. Curious Navahos drifted into camp too. Ives thought the Navahos looked like rascals, but nothing was stolen. When he gave the last of his trinkets to some Navaho squaws, the ladies were delighted. Soon after, their husbands brought to Ives enough cheese and mutton to feed the white men for a week.

The party reached Fort Defiance on May 23, and the great exploration ended. Ives was happy to find Lieutenant Tipton encamped near the fort. Two weeks later a war broke out between the Navahos and the United States troops.

Ives returned to Yuma later by Butterfield stage and sold the steamboat. For several years the *Explorer* hauled wood and freight in the Yuma area. Then she broke away from her moorings and drifted into Mexico for some exploring of her own. She was not found until 1930, when surveyors discovered the iron hull on dry land, surrounded by brush and trees.

How did the boat get on land more than a mile from the Colorado River? The answer is that the river changed its course and left the boat behind.

Powell started from the Green River bridge, seen under construction.

5. Powell Maps the Canyons

Lieutenant Ives had explored the lower Colorado River almost to the site of Hoover Dam. But for a dozen more years the upper Colorado was a twisting question mark. Strange tales were told about it. Some frontiersmen believed the river disappeared into an

41

underground passage for two or three hundred miles. Men were said to have entered this dark tunnel in boats, never to be seen again.

No one had ever gone down the Colorado from the mouth of the Green River to the Grand Canyon. Government maps showed a vast unknown territory.

One man was determined to map this desert wilderness. He was Major John Wesley Powell. In 1869, when his adventure began, Powell was 35 years old. The soft-spoken geology professor from Illinois was already well known in the west. The Indians called him Ka-pu-rats, which meant "arm off." Powell had lost his right arm in the Civil War when a Minie ball ripped into it.

Yet Powell was ready to tackle anything. He had climbed Pikes Peak with a party that included his wife, the first woman to reach the top. No lady today would climb anything higher than a stepladder in Emma Dean Powell's mountain costume. It was a one-piece dress that came down to her shoes, concealing an unknown number of petticoats.

Powell used his own savings for the Colorado trip. Scientific organizations gave him instruments and some additional money. The newly opened Union Pacific Railroad gave free transportation.

The nine other men in the party, including Powell's brother Walter, drew no pay. Several were experienced frontiersmen. One was a fugitive from the law.

Four long rowboats for the expedition were unloaded at the Union Pacific Railroad's new bridge over the Green River in Wyoming. Powell had designed the boats for rough water. Each had two watertight compartments in case of upsets in the rapids.

The Powell expedition leaving Green River in 1869. Note the old-style camera, with tripod and canvas, at left.

Bureau of Reclamation

Three of the boats were loaded with flour, beans, rice, salt pork, bacon, dried apples, coffee and sugar. There was enough food for 10 months. Powell's boat, named the *Emma Dean* for his wife, was shorter and lighter. His cargo was scientific instruments and guns.

The population of the little village of Green River cheered the voyagers when they left on May 24. After six days of smooth going they were in their first canyon. Powell named it Flaming Gorge because of the bright vermilion rocks.

The river became rougher. The roar of tumbling water was a warning of rapids ahead. If the rapids were not too bad, the men rowed through with a rush.

But when the rapids looked dangerous, the boats had to be unloaded and let down with ropes. Sometimes even an empty boat could not be trusted to the rapids. Then each boat had to be carried along the rocky bank to safe water below.

If a boat got turned sidewise while running rapids, the wave at the bottom would often upset her. The oarsmen would cling to the upside-down boat until they drifted into still water.

Powell made frequent stops to measure the altitude

and map his location from the sun and stars. Often he climbed the high walls of the canyon to get a view of the surrounding country. Hunters in the party bagged ducks, a mountain lamb and other game. The meat was a pleasant change from salt pork. By night the party camped on level spots near firewood.

On June 8 the Green River gave the explorers a warning of its power. One boat was swept over a bad rapid before the oarsmen could pull to the shore. The river slammed the boat into a rock and the three men were dumped into the water. They finally reached a sand bar in midstream and were rescued, hours later. But the boat was wrecked and a ton of food was lost. So were some of the precious barometers used to measure altitude.

The next morning John Sumner, a young trapper and expert boatman, rowed out with another man to the rocks that still held the wreckage. They found the barometers and a 3-gallon keg of whisky which had been secretly hidden in the boat. Loud cheers came from the shore when the keg was sighted. Even the stern Major had to smile, although he had first thought the cheers were for his barometers.

The wreck of one boat at Disaster Falls on the Green River.

46

The explorers hoped to get more food at the Uinta Indian reservation before they plunged into some 800 unknown miles. But food stocks on the reservation were low too. One man quit the party at this point, saying he had seen danger enough.

On July 8, Powell and George Bradley were climbing a precipice to measure the elevation at the top. Near the summit Powell found himself unable to move either up or down. He was standing on tiptoe, holding on with his single hand to a pinnacle of rock above his head. His muscles were trembling. Bradley managed to work his way to the rock above Powell but could not reach him. There was not a stick or a branch to bridge the gap. Thinking fast, Bradley took off his long drawers and lowered them. Powell grabbed the dangling legs, and Bradley pulled him up.

Shooting the rapids was a thrilling experience. Powell wrote in his journal of one good stretch on the Green River:

> Into the middle of the stream we row, and down the rapid river we glide, only making strokes enough with our oars to guide the boat. What a headlong ride it is! Shooting past rocks and

islands! I am soon filled with exhilaration only experienced before in riding a fleet horse over the outstretched prairie. One, two, three, four miles we go, rearing and plunging with the waves, until we wheel to the right into a beautiful park, and land on an island, where we go into camp.

After seven weeks of traveling the explorers suddenly came to the Colorado River. They camped several days to repair the boats and to fix the latitude and longitude. Another job was to sift 800 pounds of flour through mosquito netting. The flour had been soaked by the river and dried out many times. Some 200 pounds had to be thrown away because of hard lumps and mold.

While the party was camped at the junction, the Major saw William Hawkins, the cook, taking up the sextant. This was the instrument used for determining location by the sun and stars. Powell asked Hawkins what he was doing with the sextant. "I'm trying to find the latitude and longitude of the nearest pie," the cook said.

The Colorado proved to be much tougher than the Green. Hair-raising rapids tore the oars from the

Engraving from Powell Report

Powell's boats run a rapid—successfully.

boatmen's hands. New oars had to be sawed from driftwood. Sandy beaches were scarce. Sometimes the men slept on rocks at the foot of the canyon walls.

The boats were leaking from being thrown against rocks again and again. Coming to one of the few side canyons, Major Powell saw a chance to climb to the plateau far above. He got there and found what he was hoping for: pine trees. He cut one sleeve from his shirt, tied the end and filled it with resin to plug the cracks in the boats.

A rare piece of luck lifted every heart and comforted every stomach on July 27. Two mountain sheep were shot. Nobody ate beans or biscuits or dried apples that night. The menu was coffee and mutton and mutton and mutton.

On August 10 the tired boatmen got to the Little Colorado River. They would next enter the Grand Canyon, with far worse rapids.

The men were in poor shape for the dangers ahead. Actually they were starving. It took every ounce of strength to carry their meager supplies around bad rapids. But the Major seemed not to worry. He would make a leisurely stop of two or three days for scientific observations. What the men wanted was to get out of the gloomy canyon as fast as they could.

The last sack of flour was opened on August 26 while the party was still hemmed in by the Grand Canyon. Next day Powell and his men camped above a fearful rapid. Bradley, the man whose drawers had saved Powell on the precipice, wrote in his diary:

> The water dashes against the left bank and then is thrown furiously back against the right. The billows are huge and I fear our boats could not ride them if we could keep them off the rocks. The spectacle is appalling to us. We have only subsistence for about five days and have been trying half a day to get around this one rapid while there are three others in sight below . . . There is discontent in camp tonight and I fear some of the party will take to the mountains but hope not.

That night Powell announced that the rapid would be run in the morning. Oramel Howland took the Major aside and begged him to give up the trip. He wanted to climb out of the canyon and head for the Mormon settlements about 75 miles away. He said his younger brother and Bill Dunn would also leave.

Powell did not sleep that night. He was tempted to quit. If any lives were lost in the rapids below, it would be a terrible responsibility for him. Yet the desert above was dangerous, too.

As nearly as Powell could estimate, they should be out of the Grand Canyon within a few days. They would then be near the Virgin River, their goal. A few miles up the river they could get food from Mormon settlers.

Powell decided to stick to the river. The other five men agreed to stay with him. The Howland brothers and Dunn started up the mountain after a breakfast of biscuits, a meal "as solemn as a funeral," Powell wrote. The Major gave the three men two rifles and a shotgun. The cook gave them a pan of biscuits. Tears were shed at the parting.

The *Emma Dean* was left behind, and the other two boats got through the rapids safely. Powell's party then pulled to the shore and fired their guns as a signal that all was well. They waited two hours, hoping that the mountain climbers had heard the shots and would return. But no white man ever saw the Howlands and Dunn again.

Engraving from Powell Report

The Grand Canyon, east from Toroweap, as Powell saw it.

Two days later, after some frightful experiences with rapids, Powell and his men came out of the Grand Canyon. They feasted their eyes on the hills of the desert. No more rapids, no more portages. No more fear of being trapped a mile down.

That night, despite their hunger, the six men sat up until after midnight. They talked about the Grand Canyon and about home and about the three men who had left. Had they found a way out of the canyon? Had they found water in the desert?

The following day, August 30, the explorers came to the Virgin River. Three Mormon men and an Indian were fishing. Powell did not have to introduce himself. Word had been sent to the Mormons from their church headquarters in Salt Lake City to keep watch for any wreckage that might drift down the river. Powell's party was believed lost.

Powell checked his remaining supplies: 10 pounds of soggy flour, 15 pounds of wet apples and about 70 pounds of coffee. The Mormons quickly prepared a fine meal of fish, squash and biscuits. An Indian messenger took off for St. Thomas, 20 miles up the Virgin River, with news of the men's arrival.

The next day a Mormon bishop came from St. Thomas with a wagonload of food and other supplies, plus a packet of letters he had been holding. It was hard to decide which tasted better: the fresh bread and butter, or the first news from home in more than three months.

The party separated at the cabin of the Mormon, Joseph Asey. Powell and his brother headed for Salt Lake City for their return east. The other four men took a supply of food and started down the river again. What they wanted was a nice, easy trip to Fort Yuma.

Prairie dogs are getting scarce in the Colorado region.

6. Powell and the Indians

As Major Powell and his brother traveled up the Virgin River, they hoped for news of the Howland brothers and Bill Dunn. But there was no word until they reached Salt Lake City, more than 300 miles north. There they got a sad and puzzling message.

The report was that the three men had been found exhausted by some Shivwits Indians. The Indians fed them and showed them the trail to a Mormon settlement near St. George. On the way the men saw a squaw gathering seeds and shot her. The enraged Indians then pursued the men and killed all three.

Powell could not believe this story. He had known Oramel Howland, a printer and editor, for many years. It was impossible to think of him and his companions

Powell saw this canyon, the Wahweap, which mean Stinking Springs. The new Glen Canyon Dam on the Colorado River will flood the Wahweap.

as murderers. Furthermore, the Shivwits were a friendly tribe. Why should they have killed the men?

A year passed before Powell was able to solve the mystery. The Major had been voted $10,000 by Congress for further exploration of the Colorado country. In August 1870 he went to Salt Lake City and called on President Brigham Young of the Mormons. Powell needed a guide and interpreter to help him find a route leading down to the Colorado River from the Mormon settlements. And he hoped to get from the Shivwits the true story of his three lost men.

Brigham Young named the best man in Utah for the task: Jacob Hamblin, the Mormon scout who had spied on Lieutenant Ives 13 years before. (It must be remembered that the United States was then at war with the Mormons, and spying is part of warfare.)

Hamblin was a deeply religious man. He was trusted by the Indians and had worked for years to make peace treaties between the Indians and the Mormons. He agreed to go with Powell and his party.

The group made its camp at the upper springs of the Kanab River, about 10 miles west of the present Bryce Canyon National Park. Hamblin brought a

The Human Pickle, Powell's Indian guide.

number of Uinkaret Indians to share the camp. They promised to point out water holes, but said it was impossible to reach the depths of the Grand Canyon.

Nevertheless Powell was determined to try. He set out with a small party and soon met a guide sent to him by the Shivwits. He was "a blear-eyed, weazen-faced, quiet old man with his bow and arrows in one hand, and a small cane in the other," Powell wrote. The explorers called him "the human pickle."

The guide led them down the rock wall of a canyon, with a sheer cliff below the trail. When the ponies kicked loose stones over the edge, echoes rolled back and forth through the canyon. Finally the party reached a lower canyon—but the men were still 1,800 feet above the Colorado River.

Apparently there was no way to get down. But the Human Pickle pointed to a little shelf, so steep a man could hardly stand on it. This was the trail. But the ponies could not travel it, so they were left behind. Darkness was falling as the explorers began to work their way down a steep gulch cut into the rock by the rains of many million years.

The party halted at the edge of a chasm. A stone

tossed over the edge struck faintly, far below. It seemed there was nothing to do but wait for daylight. The Human Pickle had a better idea. He gathered a handful of dry plant stalks, tied them together and lit one end. Powell and his men made torches for themselves. Holding the torches aloft and helping each other, the men snaked their way to the bottom of the canyon. There, beside the Colorado, they made coffee and slept on a sandy beach.

The next day they found an easier way to climb up to the plateau a mile above the river.

When they got back to the main camp that night, the Shivwits came in for a council. Hamblin, Powell, the Shivwits and the Uinkarets sat around a blazing fire. Hamblin spoke first, very softly. Not a person stirred as the Mormon explained that Powell was a peaceful man, not after gold or silver.

Powell spoke next. He said that good white men wanted to know many things, and the greatest man is the one who knows most. He talked about other Indian tribes and about the people of Europe, China and Africa. He said he wanted to learn about their canyons and their mountains. Then the Shivwits chief

Engraving from Powell Report

Powell's party climbing a wall of the Grand Canyon.

answered, using Powell's Indian name of Ka-pu-rats:

Your talk is good, and we believe what you say. We believe in Jacob, and look upon you as a father. When you are hungry, you may have our game. You may gather our sweet fruits. We will give you food. We will show you the springs, and you may drink; the water is good. We will be friends, and when you come we will be glad. We will tell the Indians who live on the other side of the great river that we have seen Ka-pu-rats, and he is the Indians' friend. We are very poor. Look at our women and children; they are naked. We have no horses; we climb the rocks, and our feet are sore. We live among rocks, and they yield little food and many thorns. When the cold moons come, our children are hungry. We have not much to give; you must not think us mean. You are wise; we have heard you tell strange things. We are ignorant. Last year we killed three white men. Bad men said they were our enemies. They told great lies. We thought them true. We are very sorry.

When white men kill our people, we kill them. Then they kill more of us. It is not good.

Later, Hamblin got more facts about the tragedy from one of the Shivwits. The Howlands and Dunn had reached the Indian village almost starved. They were given food and put on the trail to the Mormon settlements. Soon after, an Indian from the east side of the Colorado arrived. He had bad news: some miners had killed a squaw in a drunken fight. Since no whites had ever come down the canyon to their village, the Indians were sure that the three men were the murderers. They followed their trail, ambushed them and shot them full of arrows.

"That night I slept in peace," Powell wrote, "although these murderers of my men, and their friends the Uinkarets, were sleeping not 500 yards away. While we were gone to the canyon, the pack train and supplies, enough to make an Indian rich beyond his wildest dreams, were all left in their charge, and all were safe; not even a lump of sugar was pilfered by the children."

The Gila
monster.

7. Where People
Are Scarce

The Colorado River drains a vast territory—272,000 square miles, an area larger than France. One-thirteenth of all the land in the United States is in the Colorado basin. But people are scarce.

They are not so scarce, however, as Lieutenant Ives predicted. He thought his men would be the last whites to visit the region south of the Grand Canyon.

Thousands upon thousands of whites have followed Ives, though seldom on the backs of starving mules. This barren region draws tourists to see the Painted Desert, the Petrified Forest, the fabulous stone arches, the cliff dwellings and other wonders.

The original settlers of the Colorado basin were, of course, the Indians. About 150,000 are still living there, mostly in Arizona and New Mexico. A map of Arizona has dotted lines marking the boundaries of Indian reservations that cover much of the state. Kaibab Indians are north of the Grand Canyon, Hualpais on the south rim. Eastward are the Navahos, Hopis and Apaches. The Mojaves are still along the Colorado River. Arizona has more Indians than any other state.

Like Indians everywhere else, those of the Colorado basin have suffered since the whites took over their country. They have been pushed out of the best land.

The white invasion began more than 400 years ago. Spanish explorers, greedy for gold, came to Arizona and New Mexico. Spanish missionaries built churches with Indian labor. But in 1680 the Indians rebelled and threw the Spaniards out.

Early in the nineteenth century the American whites began moving in, although most of the Colorado basin still belonged to Mexico. First came the trappers, traders and explorers. Next were the Mormons, seeking land for towns and ranches. Emigrants

Bureau of Reclamation (Stan Rasmussen)

Below the men on the skyline are steps carved in 1776 by Father Escalante and Father Dominquez. They made the first recorded crossing of the Colorado River at this place, the Crossing of the Fathers.

bound for the gold fields of California poured through the Colorado country in the 1850s.

Army engineers mapped routes for transcontinental railroads. Cattle men settled on grasslands.

When the Navahos and other tribes resisted the invasion, the U. S. Army was sent against them. The Indians fought well with bows and arrows. Women threw stones from the walls of canyons. But arrows and rocks were no match for rifles and field guns.

The new railroads made it possible for settlers to reach the Colorado basin comfortably. Gone were the hardships of the wagon trains pulled by plodding oxen. Towns sprang up along the railroads.

The Colorado region had its own gold rush in the last half of the nineteenth century. Silver, lead, copper and other valuable minerals were also discovered. At the Smuggler mine in Aspen, Colorado, a silver nugget weighing just over a ton set a world record. In Arizona, Henry Wickenburg's burro left camp for some prospecting of his own. Wickenburg finally overtook the stubborn animal and when the burro fled, the miner threw stones at him. The stones seemed heavier than usual. They were full of gold.

This narrow gauge excursion train posed for a picture in 1949 on the Gunnison River bridge near Cimarron, Colorado. A network of narrow gauge lines once served mines and towns of Colorado. Almost all have been abandoned, including this one.

Many prospectors perished from thirst and heat in the desert, and a number were murdered by miners who wanted to keep secret the locations of rich strikes. Cass Hite, a Civil War veteran, almost got killed for giving false directions. Hite had built a stone hut at a lonely spot on the Colorado River. He washed enough flour gold from the sand bars to buy beans, bacon and other supplies.

When other prospectors got curious about Hite's gold, he told them that all the big nuggets had been carried 60 miles down the river. Instantly a gold rush started. Dredges and ferries were hauled in sections across the rough country. Dredging began.

There was no gold. The furious prospectors went after Hite with guns, only to find his cabin empty. Hite had decided he would live longer if he stayed away from the Colorado for a couple of years.

A new kind of prospector entered the desert country after World War II. When he traveled on foot or horseback, he carried a Geiger counter. When he cruised by jeep or plane, he generally used a scintillation counter. Clicks from either instrument meant that radioactive minerals were nearby.

Some prospectors had good luck, for the Colorado plateau has probably the second largest uranium deposits in the world. But 400 pounds of ore make only a single pound of uranium oxide.

By truck and train, the ore is hauled to one of 26 mills scattered through the west, from Texas to Oregon. The mills produce uranium oxide and sell it to the U. S. Atomic Energy Commission. The federal agency manufactures pure uranium for power plants, medical research, bombs and other uses.

Santa Fe Railway (Don Erb)

Monument Valley, Arizona

8. The Desert

Many people think the desert is a place to get out of. But those who know the desert generally love it. They would not swap its multi-colored grandeur for green woods, cool streams and flower-filled swamps.

The desert is one of Nature's great treasure houses. The skyline is pierced with chains of saw-toothed

71

mountains, the highest bearing snow caps in winter. Much of the land is carved by deep canyons, yet there are broad valleys where the antelope feed. These beautiful animals bound away from the highway, white tails bobbing, and then stop to stare at the animals who drive automobiles.

The desert has extinct volcanoes, long lines of cliffs, towering buttes, miles of sand dunes, petrified forests and strange formations of rocks. And it has wonderful living things. When light rains fall in early spring, more than 700 kinds of flowering plants burst into

A coyote brings a jack rabbit to her pup at the den.
Fish and Wildlife Service (E. R. Kalmbach)

bloom. The giant saguaro cactus puts forth its waxy white blossoms. (Later the Indians will eat the purple fruits.) Flaming red flowers brighten the tall, slender stalks of the ocotillo, or candlewood.

Prairie dogs used to be seen by the dozens along the highways, but most of them have been poisoned by ranchers. Lizards run almost faster than the eye can follow them. One interesting lizard is the little horned toad, which is slow enough to catch. He shuts his eyes when stroked on top of his head. The fat and sluggish Gila monster, decorated with orange and black spots, grows up to two feet long. It is the only poisonous lizard, and the only poisonous reptile protected by law.

Where the spring rains leave small pools, the spadefoot toad lays her eggs. In two or three days the puddles are full of tadpoles. Then, if the sun doesn't dry up the water, the tadpoles quickly grow legs and lose their tails. In two weeks the young toads are ready to leave the puddle and make their way in the scorching desert. Their only water comes from the juicy insects they catch with their sticky tongues. To escape the sun, the toads dig burrows where they lie for weeks.

The desert sun is something to fear. Temperatures go up to 130° in the shade, and there is hardly any shade. Desert plants cannot have broad leaves because the sun would quickly dry them up. Leaves are tiny, and many plants—such as cactus—have none.

The greatest trader in the desert is the pack rat, which takes anything he can get his paws on. But he always leaves a pebble or piece of wood or some other small object in payment. The man who loses his wallet and gets a stone doesn't feel happy about the bargain. One pack rat dragged six sticks of dynamite from a miner's camp and finally gave up the heavy load. Following the trail, the miner jumped across a stream bed and almost landed on the dynamite.

Jack rabbits are plentiful wherever there is grass and other plant food. The jack rabbit's great enemy, the coyote, is seldom seen by men, but his wild howling is heard every night. The coyote is both smart and brave. He knows the difference between a man with a stick and a man with a gun.

The shy bighorn sheep are found in the mountains and rocky areas. They leap nimbly along narrow ledges where a man would not dare to crawl.

Fish and Wildlife Service (W. Byron Miller)

Three horned toads and one fly.

Wild burros are often seen. Because of his long drawn-out hee-haw, the burro is called "the Arizona nightingale." There are still many herds of wild horses. Their ancestors were brought to the New World 400 years ago by the Spaniards. Sadly, they have been killed by thousands for dog food and chicken food. Most of the survivors have fled to the high mesas, away from good grass and water.

Utah Tourist and Publicity Council (Hal Rumel)

Rainbow Bridge, near the Colorado River in southern Utah, is so high the Capitol could fit under it. Note the two figures on top.

Mountain lions live mainly on deer. The big cats are being slaughtered, too, because people—unlike animals—kill foolishly. One government trapper in the Grand Canyon area killed 500 mountain lions in four years and never ate one. As mountain lions become scarce, the deer multiply. Soon there are too many deer for the supply of grass. Hundreds then die slowly of starvation.

The wooded Kaibab plateau, north of the Grand Canyon, is the home of tufted-ear squirrels with white tails. This high ground is covered with pinyons and junipers. The best known animals on the plateau are a large herd of buffaloes. Fortunately they are protected against hunting.

One of the great wonders of the Colorado desert country is the huge stone arches found in several places. The locations are so rugged and lonely that hardly any of the arches were seen by white men until the twentieth century. Probably still others will be found.

The Arches National Monument, near Moab, Utah, has 88 of these natural bridges. Landscape Arch is 291 feet long, believed to be a world's record. The arches are formed from gigantic slabs of red sandstone. Over millions of years water seeped into cracks

Fish and Wildlife Service (E. P. Haddon)

Desert thief:
the pack rat.

Fish and Wildlife Service (E. P. Haddon)
The Arizona Nightingale at the Kofa Game Range, Yuma.

and loosened the slabs. Rains carried the crumbling rock, grain by grain, into the Colorado River. Desert winds kept blasting the standing slabs with particles of sand. Water and frost loosened more rock until an opening was made.

The National Park Service warns tourists not to carve initials on the rocks and not to harm plants or animals. This magnificent scenery must be enjoyed by people in the year 2000—and 3000, too.

9. The Great Flood

At the foot of California's green mountains lies a desert feared by emigrants a century ago. This is the Salton Sink, more than 200 feet below sea level.

Why so low? Because in ancient times the Salton Sink was an arm of the sea. The Gulf of California stretched some 100 miles farther north than it does today. Then the Colorado River cut the gulf in two by building a dam of silt all the way across. The upper part of the gulf became an inland lake, the present Salton Sink. After building the dam, the Colorado changed its course through the Mexican lowlands. It emptied into the gulf below the dam.

The hot sun gradually dried up the lake. Then the devil-may-care river, flooding with mountain snows,

switched its course again. It poured water and silt
into the Salton Sink until the great depression over-
flowed. Once more the river turned to the lower gulf,
and once more the inland lake dried up. But it had a
deep bed of fertile soil, brought in by the river.

In 1901 a bold project was finished. A 50-mile irrigation canal was dug from the Colorado River at
Yuma to the Salton Sink. Because the sink is far
below river level, water flowed through the canal.

The canal builders wanted to attract settlers. But
it would be hard to sell land in a scorching desert.
So they called it "The Imperial Valley."

The settlers came. They cleared the desert brush
and drew the Colorado's water from the irrigation
ditches. They planted crops, and the crops flourished.

Within three years the Imperial Valley had 10,000
people, several towns and a branch of the Southern
Pacific Railroad. The winters were like May in east-
ern United States. Crops could be planted the year
round and sold at high prices. The ranchers shipped
carloads of cantaloupes, grapes, lettuce, and other
fruits and vegetables throughout the nation.

But the Colorado River was soon up to its old

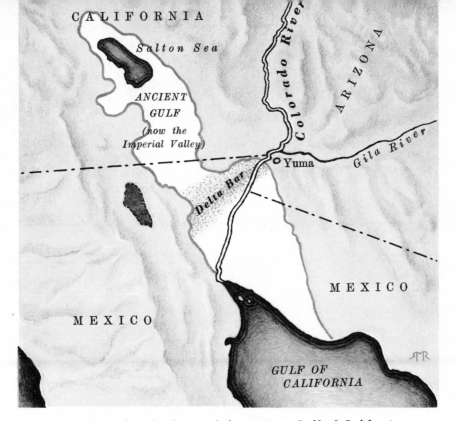

How the Colorado dammed the ancient Gulf of California.

shenanigans. First the river put so much silt into the canal that the canal couldn't carry enough water to the valley. Crops withered and died.

The canal builders were desperate. They decided to cut a new intake and bypass the silt-choked part of the old canal. This scheme worked. The valley got more water. And then an unexpected flood came down the river. Engineers tried to close the intake with brush, sandbags and piling. The wild river pushed the barrier aside and began to flow into the

The All-American Canal, before the Colorado filled it. Note size of man.
Below: Water from the Colorado irrigating a date garden.

deepest part of the Salton Sink. Unless the intake could be closed, the water would rise until it reached and covered the ranches. The Imperial valley would become a huge lake.

Could the river be stopped? The canal builders had no money for the costly battle. They appealed to President E. H. Harriman of the Southern Pacific Railroad. Harriman wired a question to Colonel Epes Randolph, head of the Southern Pacific lines in Arizona and New Mexico. "Are you certain you can put the river back into the old channel?" Harriman asked. Randolph replied that he was sure. "Go ahead and do it," Harriman telegraphed.

The first attempts failed. By December 1906, the river was tumbling through a break 1,100 feet wide and up to 40 feet deep. The railroad engineers then tried a scheme that experts said would fail too. Their plan was to build two railroad trestles across the break and fill the space between with a rock dam.

Three times the raging river tore out the 90-foot piles that had been driven for the trestles. But the bridges were finished. Meanwhile the railroad had mobilized a fleet of gondola cars and flat cars to haul

Out of bounds, the Colorado cuts a deep channel from the Salton Sink
at the rate of one foot a minute. Scene is at Calexico, California.

Above: Rock is dumped from gondola car   to dam the runaway Colorado.
Below: The break is almost closed, forcing the river back into old channel (left).

rock from quarries as far away as 400 miles. Indian workers were recruited from Arizona and Mexico.

The Southern Pacific cleared its lines for the rock trains. Heavy steam locomotives pushed the cars onto the trestles day and night. The gondola cars were dumped from the sides. Huge boulders on the flat cars were pushed overboard by work gangs. Then gravel was dumped to fill the spaces between the big rocks. Fifteen days and some 3,000 carloads after the final battle began, the river was forced back into the old channel. The valley was saved.

That year, 1907, marked the Colorado's last overflow into the Salton Sink. But the Salton Sea is still there. Water seeping underground from irrigated lands has prevented the sea from drying up.

In 1941 the All-American Canal was built from the Colorado River to the Imperial Valley. This broad canal, more than 200 feet wide, is entirely in the United States. The old canal followed an easier route through Mexico to avoid hills and sand dunes.

A century ago hardly a soul lived in the Salton Sink. Today this former desert supports more than 70,000 people—by grace of the Colorado River.

10. Damming the River

The Imperial Valley was the first big desert area turned green with water from the Colorado. Today the Colorado and its tributaries mean life to many other farm districts — and to cities too. Gigantic pumps push water from the river through pipe lines over the mountains to Los Angeles and San Diego.

Despite these good deeds, the Colorado has always meant trouble. It has clogged irrigation canals with silt. More serious, the river pours vast quantities of water into the ocean at flood stage but doesn't have enough water after the floods pass.

The federal government's Bureau of Reclamation

Two highscalers operating a wagon drill on the wall of Glen Canyon.
Holes were drilled for the left skewback of the Colorado River bridge.

This drawing shows how the Colorado was detoured into two tunnels so the dam site could be pumped dry.

has set out to change the river's habits. The Bureau intends to provide a steady, year-round flow of clean water from a river that once seemed beyond control.

A good start was made in 1936 when Hoover Dam was finished and Lake Mead was formed. The Colorado comes out of the Grand Canyon as a muddy torrent. But when the rushing water is slowed down by the vast lake, the silt falls to the bottom. The river leaves Lake Mead without its load of mud.

But Hoover Dam is not enough to tame the river. So the Bureau is now building three more huge dams to harness the upper Colorado and its main tributaries. Glen Canyon Dam, just below the Utah border, will create Lake Powell. Navaho Dam will

Glen Canyon dam site in December 1960, looking downstream. Spill-ways are high up on each rim on the canyon.

make a reservoir on the San Juan River in New Mexico, to the east. Far to the north, near the Wyoming border, Flaming Gorge Dam is being built on the Green River. A number of smaller dams on other tributaries have been started or planned.

When all of these dams are finished, the Colorado's

waters can be stored for use when needed. There will be water for thousands of dry acres. There will be water for towns and industries. And there will be an abundance of electricity from power plants at Glen Canyon, Flaming Gorge and the Gunnison River. Eventually the sales of electricity will pay back most of the money spent in building the dams.

No engineering job is more wonderful than the construction of a great dam. The Glen Canyon Dam is one of the great. When finished in 1964, it will rise 710 feet above bedrock. The new Lake Powell will back up 186 miles.

Because there were no roads at the lonely site, highways had to be built first. One paved road was laid eastward from Kanab, Utah, through 76 miles of rugged desert. Another highway was pushed north 25 miles from Bitter Springs, Arizona. But the two roads were separated by the deep gorge of the Colorado. A bridge was needed, and a bridge was built. Opened in 1959, the Glen Canyon Bridge is the highest steel arch span in the United States.

A dam site must be dry. Mud and sand must be cleared from the river bottom. Then the soft rock must be blasted away until bedrock is reached. The Glen Canyon Dam rests on bedrock more than 100 feet below the river bottom.

To dry up the Colorado at the dam site, workmen first blasted two huge tunnels in the rock walls of the canyon. Each was 41 feet in diameter—big enough to hold a 4-story house. Then a temporary dam of rocks and earth was built above the permanent dam site, and another was built below. When these coffer dams were finished, the Colorado had to make a detour through the tunnels. The space between the coffer dams was pumped dry and the excavating began.

Trucks were needed at the bottom of the gorge to bring in supplies and haul out rock. The sides of the gorge were almost vertical, with no place for a road. So the engineers dug another tunnel, two miles long, sloping from top to bottom. It was wide enough for two lanes of traffic.

A great concrete mixer was built on a shelf blasted out of the canyon wall near the top. The mixer empties wet concrete into huge buckets that travel on steel cables four inches thick. Each bucket swings

Bureau of Reclamation (A. E. Turner)

Wet concrete is dumped and tamped with compressed air at Glen Canyon Dam.

One of the two huge diversion tunnels carrying the river around the dam.

out into space and is lowered to the spot where concrete is wanted. Then the concrete is dumped.

Fresh concrete gets quite warm as it hardens. The heat from a new concrete sidewalk or highway escapes quickly into the air or ground. But the heat from huge blocks of concrete in a dam cannot get away easily. It could crack the dam.

At Glen Canyon, the fresh concrete is kept cool in two ways. First, cracked ice is used in mixing. The ice cools the hot desert sand and gravel that go into the concrete. Second, 900 miles of aluminum pipes are buried in the dam itself. Cold water is pumped through the pipes to carry away the heat and keep the concrete cool. After the dam hardens the pipes will be filled with cement.

Dam-building takes more than highways, concrete and machines. Nothing can move without men, and Glen Canyon has thousands. The town of Page was built for the workers and their families.

When the dam is finished, the diversion tunnels will be closed. The long lake will begin to rise. Already the National Park Service has planned 10 resort areas around the lake.

Motorboats will roar from one end of the lake to the other. Not many of the sightseers will remember that Major Powell took rowboats down the rapids a century ago. The rapids will have disappeared beneath hundreds of feet of water.

Three smaller dams were built on the Colorado below Hoover Dam after that high dam was finished. Imperial Dam diverts water for the All-American Canal to Imperial Valley. Parker Dam supplies water for the Los Angeles aqueduct. Davis Dam was built to generate electricity.

The Colorado is making it possible for many more people to live in the desert country. When the United States was young, the desert was thought to be a waste land forever. Daniel Webster once said:

"What do we want with this vast worthless area—this region of savages and wild beasts, of deserts and shifting sands and whirlwinds, of cactus and prairie dogs? To what use could we ever hope to put these great deserts and those endless mountain ranges, impenetrable and covered to their base with eternal snow?"

Many people agreed with Webster. They had never seen Hoover Dam or tasted an Imperial Valley cantaloupe.

Index

Meet the Author

ALEXANDER L. CROSBY was living near San Diego in 1923 when his high school principal invited him to make a trip to the Colorado desert in a Ford Model T touring car. They drove through the Imperial Valley and camped overnight on an ancient flood plain of the Colorado River. The ground was entirely covered with small, rounded stones than had been carried many miles by the river. And there was no air mattress to keep stones and bodies apart.

Although Mr. Crosby has lived in the east since 1929, he still thinks the desert is more exciting than any forest. On cross-country trips he has often stopped to explore side roads through the sage brush and cactus.

Mr. Crosby is a former newspaperman who has been a free-lance writer since 1944. He is married to Nancy Larrick, the editor of this book. The Crosbys live near Quakertown, Pennsylvania, about 2,000 miles from the headwaters of the Colorado.